MSSP
Playbook

MSSP Playbook

All rights reserved. No part of this publication may be reproduced or transmitted in any form by any means, electronic or mechanical, including photography, recording or information retrieval system, without written permission from the author.

Printed in the USA.

Copyright © 2020 Charles Henson

ISBN 13: 979-8633704600

MSSP *Playbook*

A Comprehensive Guide to Converting
Your MSP Into A
Managed Security-*Centric* Service Provider

www.msspplaybook.com
www.facebook.com/MSSPPlaybook

Charles Henson

MCSE, A+, Network+
Brentwood, TN 37027
www.CharlesHenson.net

Striving to help MSP's protect their own business
so they can learn how to better protect their clients.

A special note of gratitude:

To my favorite daughter and 11th-hour editor in crime, Leah. Thank you for the final edits and for helping me get this book complete, finally. Love you!

To my favorite son and Facebook manager, Zach, who has been instrumental in not only creating content for the future but for video editing as well. Love you!

Thanks especially to the special lady in my life, my wife Sena, for having stuck with me through thick and thin on this journey called life. Your love and support mean more to me than you will ever know. I Love you!

Scott Beck of BeckTek, my twin brother from another mother for pushing me on our one on one accountability calls every week. You've been there when I've needed to vent or help just getting through a situation.

Sandi Masori for helping me through the book launch and into International best-selling author status. You made this process easy for me.

Elaine Pofeldt for ghostwriting a portion of this book and for the first run-through of edits of my own writing.

A special note of gratitude:

Robert Boles of Blokworx for your guidance and support of the MSSP partner chapter and for always coming to the rescue when we have ghosts on the network.

Nick Espinosa Chief Security Fanatic of BSSi2 for allowing me to use his Compliance For MSP's from the Robin Robins roadshow tour. Thank you for not making me create this chapter on my own and stealing your genius!

My team at Nashville Computer who was instrumental in building out this list. Your long hours checking off all the boxes and continued focus on security have not gone unnoticed. Thank you for having each other's back, always willing to go the extra mile for our team and clients. My EPPIC Family!

Jay Ryerse of Continuum for pushing me to be more security-focused before security was cool. Your insights and guidance through the years have been invaluable.

Bo Jayakumar of Cyberstone for the cybersecurity self-assessment at the end of the book. Special thanks to you and your team for testing and auditing my MSP.

The ID Agent team for believing in me. Special thanks for allowing me to share stories, ideas and help educate the attendees at your roadshows.

A special heartfelt thank you to Robin Robins for being a leader in our industry. A woman who has helped mold me into who I am on my journey to success, in business and in life. Your resources, events, speakers, and the community you have built have influenced me more than you can ever imagine. Thank you for what you do for our community and for always being there for me!

Kerry Couch, my business partner who took a chance on me in 1991. You have influenced so many things in my life. Teaching me what a successful leader does and how he should act. Your kindness, often behind the scenes on things that even our team doesn't know about, has been inspiring. Because of you, I understand how to unselfishly give back to the community. Thank you for sticking with me through all these years and allowing me a piece of the pie!

Foreword

When you fall victim to a cybercrime attack through no fault of your own, will they call your stupid, or irresponsible?

That is the opening to a very effective lead generation marketing campaign I wrote for my MSP clients to give to their most stubborn, tight-fisted clients who refuse to put on their proverbial cybersecurity seat belt by investing in proper cybersecurity protections.

But if you are an MSP or IT services company, the same statement goes DOUBLE for you. After all, *you should know better.*

Right now, it's never been more important for any IT company – whether it's an MSP, a VAR, a solution provider or everything in between – to be focused on not only selling cybersecurity solutions but also ensuring YOUR business is locked down, putting "your oxygen mask on first" before you start to help others.

My company, Technology Marketing Toolkit, Inc., runs the world's largest C-level peer group for MSPs and serves over 5,000 clients internationally, with a subscriber database of over 40,000. As such, I've seen MANY smart, professional, and competent MSPs have their entire world undone when they get hit with ransomware or some other cyber-attack.

One client, who will remain nameless, had a rogue tech delete all of their clients' data, several of which were hospitals and medical facilities. Was the client able to restore all the data? Yes, he did. Was he insured? Yes, he was. But the costs of the breach were so high that they far exceeded his policy and (of course) personal ability to pay. As you can imagine, his clients were infuriated by the giant, costly, business-interrupting crisis he inflicted on them. Their reputations were damaged, their businesses significantly interrupted.

The devastating stress it put on him, along with the worry, anxiety and GUILT he felt for exposing his clients, was his undoing. His health suffered. His family suffered. His employees suffered. He wound up in near financial ruin – all because of one incident.

This is just ONE story among hundreds. More of this is going on than you think, covered up and hushed by the companies it's happening to, for fear of lawsuits, the irrevocable bad reputation it would cause and loss to their IT services business.

If you are a true professional and fiduciary to your clients, you would be stupid AND irresponsible to not read this fantastic book by my long-term client and friend Charles Henson. He has been a leader for many of the peer groups we run, as well as an advisor to various vendors on the topic of securing your own MSP. I urge you to not only read this, but to enact his advice and then use that as a marketing "wedge" to knock out incumbent competitors who simply refuse to take this matter as seriously as they should.

-Robin Robins

Table of Contents

A special note of gratitude: iv
Foreword vii

Preface xi
Chapter 1   Cybersecurity Warfare 1
Chapter 2   NSA Tools For Sale 7
Chapter 3   Understanding Your Liability 15
Chapter 4   MSP Lockdown: Securing Your MSP 19
Chapter 5   Vendor Management And Selection 21
Chapter 6   Building Your Security Stack:
            What MUST Be Included 23
Chapter 7   Common Sense Security And Basic Policies 37
Chapter 8   Steps To Better Protect Your MSP .41
Chapter 9   Enable Multi Factor Authentication on
            EVERY Login, EVERY Portal 49
Chapter 10 Factoring In Other Security Concerns 61
Chapter 11 Why Partnering With An MSSP Is Necessary 67
Chapter 12 Third Party Validation 75

Chapter 13 New Security Breach Notification Laws:
           What You Need to Know............................79
Chapter 14 Complying with Compliance 83
Chapter 15 Going to Market 91

Bonus Material:..121
A Final Word...125
About the Author 127
Charles Henson...127

Preface

Seventy percent of people who read a book do not take action. If you read or hear something in this book that you intend to act on, take notes, put a date next to your notes, and then take action! The best ideas, strategies, processes, and knowledge all do you no good without action!

Knowledge is not power.
Execution of the knowledge is where the power lies.

– Tony Robbins

As an MSP (managed service provider), I struggle with the fact that our clients are under attack all day, every day. We ourselves are under siege. Thanks to Operation Cloudhopper and Sam Sam attacks, MSPs are now falling victim to attacks with their entire client base and networks being infected and shut down by cybercriminals. To date, we know of over 300 MSPs that have had ransomware infect their entire client base because of an insecurity within the MSPs themselves! With the growing threats and dangers that are out there, more and more companies are getting hit. You probably know about the Marriott breach, which exposed more than 500 million customers' data. LinkedIn, Twitter, Snapchat, Slack, and Adobe have also been hit.

These are all large companies, but the bad guys don't just attack the bigger targets. MSPs own the keys to the kingdoms of thousands of small businesses. By hacking one MSP, the hackers are gaining access to multiple small and medium businesses and setting off ransomware in the hopes that some or all of them will pay the ransom. Larger organizations can afford a more extensive IT security budget and throw money at security solutions to better protect themselves, but you and I have to increase our spending on newer technology safeguards while our margins get tighter.

This is why I'm writing this book. We need to not only know how to protect ourselves but also how to protect our clients. It's not about the clients getting a virus anymore. It's about hackers gaining access to their systems and using their systems for their own malicious deeds and financial gain. In the past, it was more about malicious acts such as a rootkit or a virus that infects your system just to shut it down. Today's threats are much more targeted: whether they are used for ransomware, so the files are useless until you pay the ransom, or they are deployed to gain access to your systems and client data so that criminals can sell the information they have obtained on the Dark Web. One MSP I know of was shocked to see its credentials and back-end access to its systems for sale on the Dark Web.

Preface

Against this backdrop, many MSPs struggle with what to do next in the security space. Often, when you don't have a large budget, it's hard to think about implementing something that might cost hundreds of thousands of dollars. Additionally, we don't have the time or resources to vet these various tools, test them, deploy them, and then verify cohesiveness across all clients.

That's where this book comes in handy. I'm going to walk you through what we have done successfully, as well as what has worked for many other MSPs in building out a security stack. You'll learn how to vet essential security vendors, what dangers to look out for, how to eliminate the need to hire a six-figure security engineer, and instead find a strategic partner(s) who has already hired, trained and staffed the SOC (security operations center).

We'll also cover what's happening on your clients' networks without your knowledge. If you don't have the right security stack in your clients' network, then I am willing to bet that malicious activity is happening right now. Ever have accounts get locked out, but you don't know why? Is the WMI broken and causing AD to be corrupted? Are clients' IPs landing on blacklists without you even noticing? These are all indicators that this may be occurring. We also found sites with crypto miners running, as well as hosts serving up ransomware payloads. Would you know if a crypto-miner was running on your network? The old days of a virus hitting your system with the aim of shutting it down are nearing their end. Now, its hackers gaining access to systems, going undetected and using yours and your client's systems for their financial gain.

When you install the proper tools, you will identify threats that you never knew were there before. We all need to step up our game as MSPs and defend our clients from the hackers and scammers who are bringing on threats at an exponential rate. In the pages to come, I will show you the essentials to building out your MSSP (managed security-centric service provider) in a way that gives you 100% confidence you are doing all you can to protect your MSP and your clients.

Chapter 1

Cybersecurity Warfare

This is not a story about ransomware. This is not about viruses, or Trojans, or rootkits. What we're looking at today is how hackers are gaining access to systems and the real threat that is out there. Our clients' networks are not being protected. Our MSPs themselves are under attack. The APT10 group running Operation Cloud Hopper, along with the Chinese government, was after our credentials, and it's not just these groups. If, through whatever means it takes, a hacker can gain access to an MSP's credentials, then they know that they have access to all of our clients. We have to take measures not only to protect ourselves as individuals, our businesses, and also our clients' businesses but also to educate our clients on how to better protect their businesses through technology and education.

There are countless cases now where hackers have been inside of computer systems, undetected, for months at a time. The Democratic Party suffered from this during the 2016 election. In Atlanta, an orthopedic center experienced an attack where the hackers were in the system for months. The hackers set off ransomware from within the network, and even though the orthopedic center had good backups to restore its data, the hackers demanded that they pay the ransom, or their medical records would be released. The center did not pay the ransom, and the hackers then released 8,000+ medical records, doubled the ransom, and threatened to then release more if they didn't pay. Think about the implications here. The center paid the ransom, but they could not assure patients that the data was actually destroyed. It was most likely put up for sale within the Dark Web across multiple sites.

Siphoning data out of networks is nothing new. This happened with a breach at Uber that the company initially denied. We later learned that Uber paid hackers more than $100,000 to *supposedly* delete the data. Did the data actually get deleted? I guarantee you, as with the orthopedic center, they actually did not delete the data, even though they told Uber that they would upon being paid. Why would they delete data that they could sell again, multiple times over in the future? After all, these were criminals that stole the data to begin with… Not the most ethical people on the planet!

In another case, hackers had been in a law firm's system for more than nine months and had changed all of the backups to back up only a few directories so that the backups wouldn't be getting errors. The MSPs didn't notice that the amount of data being backed up had changed. Policies and procedures were not in place to double-check those backups. Test restores were not performed during those nine months, and when the hackers had gained access to all of the data that they had wanted, they were ready to move forward with their attack. When they released the ransomware on their systems, it was over a holiday weekend so that the encryption would have time to encrypt the entire data set without being stopped or noticed.

The company had to pay the ransom because it had no backups. It took them more than nine days to un-encrypt their data. They were fortunate once they paid the ransom that the keys to un-encrypt the data actually worked. The FBI and CIA had both mentioned at their 2019 Ransomware Nationwide roadshow that some hackers were not delivering the un-encryption key even after being paid.

We had a case at our company where a prospect called us for help. Their manufacturing firm had no backups in place. It had been a break-fix client that didn't value what its IT company offered them and had felt that they never needed such a service, so why install one now? Then a user received an email containing a link that set off ransomware. Once he clicked on that link, the ransomware attack started encrypting the company's data. Because this prospect didn't have any backups in place, it decided to pay the ransom. Once they paid (and while we were still extracting the data and decrypting it), they fell for another ransomware attack via e-mail, thus encrypting the encrypted files and making their data irrecoverable. That company has since closed its doors, and the plant sits empty today.

You must take precautionary steps and put them in place to protect your clients. All it takes is a single mouse click inside of a malicious email or a visit to an infected website and a client, or even one of your employees, can give a hacker remote access to that machine. You owe it to your clients and employees to defend them to the best of your ability, or to let someone else do it. There is a lot at stake when an MSP gets attacked.

In California, an MSP was using a version of a software that had not been patched or updated on several clients' machines. Hackers gained access and exploited this vulnerability in the software, gaining control of the workstations where the software was installed. The hackers ran scripts across multiple client machines and set off ransomware that encrypted all files, on all devices, across the entire network of every client with the unpatched software. It took more than a month for the MSP and a volunteer team of other MSPs to re-setup all of the servers so that they could restore the data across all clients. Fortunately, the MSP had all of its clients backed up, and the hackers didn't touch the backups. Do you have ALL your software(s) patched?

In Tennessee, hackers had used an online portal to gain access to two racks of servers that an MSP managed and were able to gain access to every server hosted on the cloud infrastructure. They infected the entire structure with ransomware and then demanded a ransom of $1.2 million. The owner of the MSP did not have the money to pay them and didn't have cybercrime insurance. Because the hackers deleted them, there were no backups to restore the files and the MSP's clients lost their data, exposing the MSP to legal liability. The MSP's website, soon after, went offline and its phone number was taken out of service. What would you do if all of your clients were infected at once?

In Georgia, an MSP neglected to close RDP on an internal server. Hackers used brute force to get in and listed the access to the MSP for sale on the Dark Web. The access was put up for sale for a measly $600. Luckily, a security company within the industry found the listing and was able to obtain the IP addresses of the breached server. The security company contacted the MSP to warn them of the breach and they closed RDP and changed all passwords across all systems. Fortunately, they dodged a bullet, but many MSPs are not so lucky.

These situations all took place recently. Hackers are getting more and more aggressive by the day, and they've found that attacking MSPs can be very profitable. Not only can they breach your technology systems, but they can also hack into the data of your customer base. Hackers who want to steal data from big companies' supply chains are well aware that MSPs, which are increasingly involved in supporting them, are often the weakest link. MSPs that fail to put the appropriate security in place are risking serious liability.

Many MSPs are so busy that they neglect taking basic steps to protect themselves and think that they'll be able to withstand these risks if they have insured themselves. Even if you have cyber insurance and E&O insurance (Errors & Omissions), you still have to take reasonable care to protect your own systems and clients' data. Otherwise, you will find yourself in the same predicament as a fine jewelry store owner who can't collect on a claim after a robbery because he didn't keep his merchandise locked away after hours. In many cases, MSPs are unable to obtain cyber liability.

Unfortunately we are unable to quote XXXX Consulting Services, inc.

After further review of the application and underwriting information, we are not able to offer coverage to XXXX Consulting Services, inc. at this time. The reason for this declination is:

Our security scan has detected that the domain provided may be associated with a Managed Service Provider (MSP). We have threat intelligence and claims data suggesting that MSPs are being targeted extensively by hackers to push ransomware to all of their clients. Due to elevated risk conditions in this industry, Coalition is not able to issue a policy at this time.

Insurance Companies Are Declining To Sell MSPs Insurance

Mastering the latest security strategies isn't just about avoiding risk. It's also about finding opportunities for growth. Many MSPs are being asked to take on increased responsibilities for keeping clients' data safe. For instance, some IT teams are asking MSPs to support them with dark web monitoring to make sure that their data isn't being sold. MSPs that know how to utilize the proper tools have a chance to deepen their role as strategic partners. MSP owners also have an opportunity to create educational programs such as webinars that can bring revenue into their business.

Let's take a look at some of the tools that the hackers are using today to attack both our clients and us.

Chapter 2

NSA Tools For Sale

In 2016, the NSA (National Security Agency) was hacked by Chinese Intelligence Agents and its toolset compromised. The hackers were able to access the NSA's devices and used the tools against the agency, much like a gun being taken out of the hands of one criminal and used by another criminal that grabbed it. The hackers offered the tools to the highest bidder, and when they didn't get the dollar amount that they were after, they changed to an auction-style sale of the tools and offered them for a discounted rate to thousands of other hackers…

The Department of Homeland Security has worked with Australia, Canada, New Zealand, and the United Kingdom Security Authorities to identify some tools being used for malicious purposes in recent cyber incidents around the world.

The following are some types of tools that you should consider defending against. There is an exhaustive list, but we don't have space to add them all here. These tools and the alerts have been seen and used to compromise information across a wide range of businesses, including healthcare, finance, government, and defense companies. The widespread availability of these tools presents a challenge for network defense and threat attributes.

These tools fit into the five categories:

1. Remote access Trojans, (RAT).
2. Web shells
3. Credential stealers
4. Lateral movement frameworks
5. Command and control (C2)

Let's talk about each of these tools briefly and look at how they're being used.

Remote Access Tools (RAT)

First on the list is the remote access Trojan. RAT is a program that, once installed on a victim's machine, allows remote administration and control. In a malicious context, it can, among many other functions, be used to install backdoors, key loggers, take screenshots, run scripts, view the camera of the compromised device, and extract data.

Malicious remote access tools can be difficult to detect because they are normally designed to appear in a list of running programs and services and can mimic the behavior of legitimate applications. This tool is used with the purpose of delivering malicious attacks against the victim, either by gaining remote access for further exploration or stealing their valuable data, such as credentials/passwords, banking credentials, intellectual property, or PII (private identifiable information).

Possible indicators of a remote access tool are:

(1) the inability to restart the computer in safe mode,

(2) an inability to open the registry editor as well as task manager,

(3) a significant increase in disk activity and/or network traffic,

(4) an uptick in connection attempts to non-malicious internet protocols and addresses, and

(5) the creation of new files and directories with odd and/or random names.

The best ways to prevent breaches via remote access tools is by turning off RDP, as well as educating clients against phishing email attacks, and installing a spam filter that checks the link within the email to verify it is not going to download a malicious payload. In the event a client machine has a RAT installed, the hacker can manipulate Active Directory, escalate privileges, and control the machine without you or the user knowing they are there.

Web Shell

Number two on our list is Web Shell, aka China Chopper. This well-documented, publicly available web shell has been widespread since 2012. It runs malicious scripts that are uploaded to a target host after initial compromise and grants a threat actor/hacker remote administrative capability. Once the access is established, web shells can be used to pivot to additional hosts within a network.

This threat has been extensively used to remotely access compromised web servers, where it provides group policy and directory management, along with access to the virtual terminal and compromised devices. China Chopper is a 4k file and is an easily modifiable payload. Detection and mitigation are difficult for definition-based network defenders.

Two main components of this are:

(1) the client-side, which is run by the attacker, and
(2) the China Chopper server, which is installed on the victim's web server and is also controlled by the attacker. The web shell client installs terminal commands and managed files on the victim's server. Its MD 5 hash is publicly available online.

The web shell server can easily be uploaded in plain text and is changed by the attacker, which makes it harder to define the specific hash as they can't be identified adversely by traditional antivirus. Once a server has this web shell, it can be used to upload or download and manipulate files and data on the webserver, including editing, deleting, copying, renaming, and even changing the timestamps of existing files.

The biggest way to avoid getting compromised is to ensure that your server is not running on a public-facing web server and is up to date with the latest security patches applied.

While the China Chopper web shell server upload is in plain text, commands issued by the client base-64 are encoded. They are easily decode-able. However, the TLS (transport layer security) by web servers has resulted in web server traffic becoming encrypted, making detection of China Chopper activity using network-based tools more challenging. The most effective way to detect and mitigate China Chopper is on the host itself. Specifically, on public-facing web servers, there are simple ways to search for the presence of the web shell using the command line on both Linux and Windows-based operating systems.

Although it wasn't intended as a hacking tool in recent years, multiple bad actors/hackers have used the web shell for malicious purposes. Its use against companies around the world has prompted organizations worldwide to reevaluate their network defenses. Hackers typically use this web shell to gain access to a host and to move throughout the internal network without being detected. Once the tools are on the network and the hackers gain access, they can get administrator privileges, escalate privileges within a domain, and perform sideways attacks on other devices. We will talk more about how to understand privilege escalation in the checklist section of this book.

Lateral Movement Credential Stealers

PowerShell Empire

The third tool on our list is PowerShell Empire. This is a lateral movement tool designed to allow an attacker to move around a network after gaining initial access. It can be used to generate malicious documents and executables for social engineering access to the network. This framework was designed as a legitimate penetration-testing tool in 2015.

PowerShell Empire acts as a framework for continued exploitation once a hacker has gained access to the system. It gives the hacker the ability to escalate privileges, harvest credentials, extract information, and move laterally across a network. It is a powerful exploitation tool because it's built on a common, legitimate application, PowerShell, and can operate almost entirely on memory. It can be very difficult to detect on a network using traditional antivirus tools.

PowerShell has become increasingly popular among hackers and organized criminals. This is the same tool used in the Winter Olympics data breach. Social-engineered emails, malicious attachments, and a spear-phishing campaign came from South Korea's organizations. The attack had multiple layers of sophistication, and it was almost undetectable due to its use of a PowerShell script.

Detecting malicious PowerShell activity is almost impossible because it is a standard operating procedure. It is best to follow Microsoft PowerShell security practices. We will also discuss how to allow only whitelisted PowerShell scripts within your Advanced Endpoint Protection in the checklist section of this book.

Command and Control C2

Attackers use command and control, aka C2, to disguise their location when compromising a target, making it very hard to determine where the root connection is and to identify malicious traffic going out to the hacker's network. The HUC packet transmitter, aka H Tran, is a proxy tool that has been used since 2009 to intercept and redirect TCP (transmission-controlled protocol) packets, from a localhost to a remote host.

This makes it possible for the attackers to hide their communications with the victim's network. The H Tran facilitates TCP connections between the victim and a hop point controlled by the hacker. Malicious hackers can use this technique to redirect their packets through multiple compromised hosts, running H Tran to gain greater access to a host in a network. We've seen this both in government, as well as in industry attacks. It can be used to evade intrusion and detection systems on networks, blend in with common traffic, and leverage domain trust relationships to bypass security tools. It can also be used to hide the command and control infrastructure, hide communications, create peer-to-peer or meshed command, and control infrastructure to evade detection providing resilient connections to infrastructure.

We personally have seen this attack break WMI and corrupt the active directory on clients' networks. We ended up having to use a wide range of tools to detect where the threat was actually hiding and on which machine. We ended up rebuilding the clients' Active Directory from scratch. This tool is commonly installed when a user clicks on a link within an email. The malicious hacker immediately has control of the device and, using this tool, will not be detected without having a SIEM (security information event monitoring) or another network monitoring device, such as an enterprise firewall, within the network.

This is the type of attack that, as I mentioned in the preface, is most likely already within your clients' networks. You will have no idea that the hackers have gained access and won full control of the back end of your clients' systems because the network traffic blends in with the rest of your web, internet traffic, and ports 53, 443, & 3306. It is nearly impossible to detect because these services are common protocols flowing through our clients' networks.

To avoid this type of attack, you should apply security patches and prevent RDP from being opened. Also, educate your users not to click on links and install a SIEM-type service to ensure that you see this type of activity on your clients' networks.

These are just a few of the tools used to attack us and our clients' networks. The US Department of Homeland Security has posted an extensive list of protective measures online. We must put these in place to protect our companies and our client's businesses from these types of attacks.

In light of the tools above, it's time to take action to become an MSSP, instead of just taking care of your clients from a break-fix aspect or turning a blind eye to our own network security. If you are not talking to your clients and educating them on the dangers of these tools and many other threats, then your competition will and you will be losing clients in the months ahead.

Chapter 3

Understanding Your Liability

Do you have clients who decline your managed services, and then months later argued that you take care of all of their IT for them? Unfortunately, we used to have this discussion from time to time with our own clients, and it was usually uncomfortable. We had to remind the client that they opted to not pay for our higher-end services, which include monitoring and management of their network.

Disclaimer here: I'm not an attorney or an insurance broker. This is one MSP owner talking to another.

It is essential to have E&O, insurance, as well as cyber insurance to protect your managed services business. Be sure to sit down with your clients and educate them on the types of tools and security dangers that are out there and why they too, need to have cybercrime insurance.

We have recently updated our master client agreement to say that the client is required to have cyber liability insurance. We've also had a discussion with our E&O insurance agent, as well as increased our cyber liability coverage. Our insurance company used a perfect analogy to explain why this is necessary. You can go into any jewelry store during the day, and it will be beautifully lit, with wide-open windows and everything out on display. At the end of the day, if you drive by, you'll notice that there are bars on the windows and doors, as well as roll-up doors and roll-up windows. If you peer inside, the cases will be empty and no jewelry will be visible. There will be metal gates covering the entrance and all of the windows so that thieves, or would-be thieves, cannot get inside.

Do you know that if a jewelry store does not take the proper measures to secure its valuables that the insurance company will not cover their claim in the event of theft? That is the reason jewelry stores use the precautions above.

This is the type of story to share with your clients. It is up to us to educate our clients on the need to talk with their insurance agent and let them know the dangers that are out there, the tools that are available, and the services that we can use to help them defend against hackers and cybercriminals at various price points. Additionally, you and your clients cannot rely on an insurance policy alone. You will need to do your due diligence to ensure you are putting policies in place as well as following the best practices to protect your devices and educate your employees.

If they do not want to take these measures, it is highly recommended that you obtain a "decline of service" letter. See the bonus section at the end of the book for a sample "decline of service" letter.

If a client declines buying into your managed services and paying you to install the tools required to protect their network from cyber attacks, you should have them sign this and keep it on file so that you have proof of discussion in the event that they get breached.

I am not an attorney, nor do I play one on the Internet. Speak with your attorney. Get legal advice and talk to your insurance broker for recommendations on what to put in place to protect yourself and your clients.

Now, think about the jewelry store analogy and ask yourself if you are taking the proper measures to lock-down your MSP. Do you have policies and procedures in place? Multi-factor authentication on EVERY software or portal that you use?

Hackers are getting more aggressive and devious by the day, but there is no reason for MSPs or their clients to be victimized. Assembling the right security stack can prevent common breaches such as hacking into RDP or phishing, where hackers trick someone into clicking on a link they've sent and get remote access to a company's technology systems.

Unfortunately, there are countless claims filed with insurance companies that go rejected and unpaid by insurance companies due to the lack of due diligence in securing a company's network. By taking measures to better protect your MSP as well as your clients, you will be better equipped to fight for the claim to be approved and paid by showing that you are practicing the best practices. Furthermore, you owe it to your clients to ensure they know the dangers of turning a blind eye to security and assuming that the insurance coverage they have will cover anything that happens without question. Here is yet another conversation you could be having to educate your client and stand out from your competition.

Chapter 4

MSP Lockdown: Securing Your MSP

Put YOUR oxygen mask on before helping your clients with theirs!

If you have ever flown on an airplane, you are aware of the flight attendants going through the safety features while traveling on the aircraft. One particular security instruction is on how to use the oxygen mask if cabin pressure should drop, and the oxygen masks fall from the compartment above. The instructions detail how to put the mask on properly and make it tight, but the one thing to pay attention to is that you should put your own mask on prior to assisting others, even your infant. Now let's be honest; this seems cruel. However, it is impossible for you to help your child or infant if you have passed out from oxygen deprivation. These instructions are to ensure that you are receiving oxygen and are available to help others. I use this analogy with securing your MSP because if you yourself get hacked and your tools are inaccessible, can you really help your clients?

The answer is no. Let's take a look at how to properly put that oxygen mask on before we continue. What elements should your security stack include? It helps to look at the building process the same way you might think about protecting your home from intruders.

If you really want to make sure your home is secure, you'll take several steps—not just one or two. For instance, you might start securing your house by putting locks on the doors and windows and a fence around the perimeter of your house. Then you might get a watchdog that stands guard in the yard and install both a burglar alarm and security cameras. Maybe there is a gun or baseball bat next to the bed…

You might use a similar multi-layered approach at an office building. There may be a fenced-in parking lot outside with security cameras in the parking lot, a security guard who verifies visitors' identities by looking at their driver's license, and another security guard making his rounds within the perimeter. Then, inside the building there may be another security guard who does a second check of a visitor's driver's license. The guard then calls the person the visitor is meeting with to make sure it's okay to buzz them in, or slide a key fob within the elevator and pushes the floor number on the visitor's behalf.

Taking this same multi-step approach is important within your own MSP. Once you have your systems on lockdown, you will have a major competitive advantage over the many MSPs that operate like a cobbler who has no shoes.

Chapter 5

Vendor Management And Selection

Within my MSP, I do not decide to go with a new vendor or new product without enlisting the help and advice of my team. I want to empower them, allow them to collaborate, and discuss the various tools that can best be used to protect our clients. I also encourage them to watch webinars, attend product demos, and compare with their peers the products they feel will best safeguard our clients and fit within our company structure.

If you do not have a team of employees that you can collaborate with, I highly recommend that you join a Facebook group of MSPs and IT service providers and have discussions with them on how to choose a vendor, as well as which vendors they currently have chosen and why. It is easy today with social media to collaborate with others and not have to be on an island all on your own.

Empowering your team to help you decide which tools are best for your clients allows them to buy into the tools themselves, take ownership, and make sure that those tools are successful. It ensures that your clients stay safe because they will have a vested interest in ensuring that the decision that they helped make was the right one.

You have a decision to make between training your staff and outsourcing what you cannot or do not want to handle. If you're trying to build out a SOC (security operating center), this is most likely more than you can financially handle within your MSP. I would recommend that you look at companies for specific services and partner with them, so that you may outsource the burden and heavy cost of highly-skilled engineers and continue to focus on what you do best.

Now, let's take a look at building and assembling your stack. We'll discuss the types of products you and your team should be looking at, how they are able to help protect you and your clients, and the differences between them.

Chapter 6

Building Your Security Stack: What MUST Be Included

Recommended Security Stack for Every MSP:

NextGen Firewall	SIEM	DarkWeb Monitoring	Written Policies & Procedures
2FA	RMM	Advanced End Point	Breach Detection System
DNS Filtering	Cyber Insurance	E&O Insurance	Backups
SPAM Filter	Security Training	Threat Actor Activity	Enforced Security Policies

The Fence

Next generation firewall edge protection: A good firewall is your first line of defense against data loss. A firewall configured with DLP (data loss prevention) will alert you and remove information that is traveling out of the network that should not be—like social security numbers, credit card data, or other PII (personally identifiable information) sent in a plain text email or document attachments. When the firewall detects this type of transfer, it will intercept it and prevent the information from leaving the system if configured properly.

You can partner with an MSSP that operates a SOC and allow your firewall syslogs to feed into their systems so that they can alert you in the event of malicious activity within your networks or your clients'. In a few cases where we had ghost-like activity, our only tool to find the attack was via firewall logs fed to a backend SIEM. There are many enterprise level firewalls that have these capabilities and clients are willing to spend the additional money for better protection. You, as an MSP, should also invest in this type of firewall for your own network.

You also want to make sure that you have a UTM (unified threat management) in place, as well as a virtual private network, web content filtering, multi-wide area networks, intrusion detection, and prevention systems enabled on the firewall. If you decide to use a VPN, ensure that it too uses multifactor authentication.

The Guard Dog

Breach detection system: This is made up of software tools that search for hackers' techniques that have slipped past conventional security systems. Footholds within the operating system can go undetected by legacy definition-based anti-virus software. Once the hacker has access to the PC, he can inject a known, well-running service with a persistent infection that allows remote access even after a PC is restarted.

The Surveillance Cameras

Security information event management (SIEM): SIEM software is a combination of SEM (security event management) and SIM (security information management), which is capable of monitoring threats, providing real time security alerts, and increasing compliance. On its own, SEM centralizes interpretation and storage of logs; and SIM collects data to be analyzed for reporting. When combined, you get the full terminology, SIEM, which combines these two systems together to provide fast analysis and identification of security events in real-time, and analysis of security alerts generated by applications and network hardware. The data is aggregated from many sources, including network, security devices, servers, databases, and applications. It provides the ability to consolidate monitored data to help avoid missing crucial events. SIEM visibility and anomaly detection could help detect zero-days or polymorphic code. Beyond this, alerts of data breaches can be detected by a SOC monitoring these alerts.

Door and Window Locks

Advanced endpoint protection: Traditional definition based anti-virus is dead! Not only does it leave your company exposed, but it also leaves your clients open to zero-day attacks. Migrating to a behavior-based, advanced endpoint protection suite allows you to have zero-day protection as it is machine learning. Some more advanced tools include using AI (artificial intelligence) to determine if the activity of an attached or opened file is performing malicious activity. If the activity seems malicious, the tools stop the execution and prevent the program from starting. These newer tools help to protect computers, servers, laptops, and even most tablets, mobile phones, and other portable devices. Ensure that your advanced endpoint protection is capable of script blocking. Yes, script blocking...

I understand that most RMM tools have countless scripts, and most anything you do on a system requires PowerShell. It is critically important that you whitelist any script that is required to be run by your RMM tool, as well as any PowerShell script one off's that are necessary. RMM tools have been known to have security flaws, and if script blocking isn't enabled, you could be the victim of the next flaw. Take the steps - and yes, there are a lot of steps, and it requires a lot of time, but I cannot urge you enough to get this done for every client!

The Alarm-Monitoring Service

Remote monitoring and management (RMM): Every MSP should have remote monitoring and management systems. These tools allow you to access your clients' systems remotely. Tools such as Kaseya offer rapid remote control, patching, automation, and integration with the OS that allow you to perform tasks remotely on every PC and server that you manage. Inventory asset control, application deployment, and patch management are just a few of the many advantages of utilizing an RMM.

The Motion Detection System

Threat actor activity: This refers to security monitoring of the Administrator account and user escalation of privileges added to a user, along with new user creation alerting. Ever see a rouge user with full admin rights, but don't know when or who created it? Choose software that keeps you posted on any potential internal security issues going on inside your network and your clients. It should either be real time, or at least configured for a set time for the daily scan, and report back with an email or ticket alert sent to any address you specify or your ticketing system. The daily alerts aggregate the issues that were detected during the past 24 hours and can be sorted either by priority/severity (high, medium, or low) of the threat, or by the type of issue (threat, anomaly, or change). It is always good to know if and when a user account gets created, as well as who got upgraded to an admin. This tool is a must for not only your network, but every client you manage.

The Roaming Security Officer

DNS filtering: DNS filtering, aka security Internet gateway, provides better visibility and control for internet traffic. By using a DNS filter, all Internet traffic is verified as being from a good, known source. Using DNS filtering reduces the number of threats that are permitted in your environment significantly and improves performance by enabling secure, direct-to-internet access. We saw a 30% reduction in help desk calls when we implemented this service across our own client base.

The Owner's Manual

Security awareness training: At an FBI and CIA roadshow in Nashville, the presenters stated that 90% of the cases they work could have been prevented with user training. We can put every tool and security measure in place, but as soon as a hacker persuades a user to give up their username and password via an e-mail link, all of our hard work is out the door! We need to ensure that our staff, as well as our clients, are being educated on the latest threats and typical ways hackers are gaining access. It takes place via not only e-mail, but also over the phone, using social engineering, or even by a person walking through our front door. Once you have trained your staff, send a phishing e-mail to see who opens the e-mail and who clicks on the link. It is better to test your staff, and if they click on the links, to teach them the dangers before they clink on an actual infection.

The Flood Lights

Backup and disaster recovery: When all else fails, restore from backup! Backups should be running throughout the day and sent offsite every evening. It is recommended that you back up all servers using a file-level backup. In the event of a disaster, ransomware attack, or other data loss, you can restore the data back to the same or another server. Data backups must be offsite as well in case you or your client has an event that causes the building or devices to be lost or damaged.

The Intercom System

E-Mail filtering and backups: Today, business depends on e-mail as the number one communication tool. You want to make sure that you have email encryption, email archiving, email backups, and spam filtering. Hackers can now encrypt a user's inbox with ransomware, leaving the message sender and subject line readable to remind you of the importance of the e-mail, and thus enticing you to pay the ransom. Furthermore, since SPAM is the number one attack method, you should always use a SPAM filter and ensure e-mail traffic cannot be sent directly to the server. The server should only accept e-mails from the filtering service. With newer based technology, some SPAM filters have the ability to test links in a sandbox and ensure that the link in the e-mail is not malicious or linked to a dangerous payload. Ensure that every client has this service.

The Deadbolt

Enforced security policies: Security protocol, at a minimum, should include lockout policies for account password failure. Three failed login attempts, and the user account should be locked! This will eliminate brute force attacks and slow down someone who is trying to guess a user's password. We have seen countless attacks where the hacker used brute force and a dictionary or passwords to ultimately break into a secured network system, all because a lockout policy was not in place. This is one of the easiest ways to defend against brute force attacks.

The Biometric Scanner

Dark Web monitoring: We can do a dark web scan for a domain name to identify whether there is PII, as well as usernames and passwords that belong to a client's domain name.

You need to tell clients that if they are using any third party sites with a username and password, all passwords should be unique for each site. This is a great time to educate your team and your clients never to use the same password twice. Here is some additional information in regard to dropping password change policies from Microsoft's site: shorturl.at/cfmN7

* * *

"Dropping the password expiration policies."

"There's no question that the state of password security is problematic and has been for a long time. When humans pick their own passwords, too often, they are easy to guess or predict. When humans are assigned or forced to create passwords that are hard to remember, too often, they'll write them down where others can see them. When humans are forced to change their passwords, too often, they'll make a small, predictable alteration to their existing passwords and/or forget their new passwords. When passwords or their corresponding hashes are stolen, it can be difficult at best to detect or restrict their unauthorized use.

"Recent scientific research calls into question the value of many long-standing password-security practices such as password expiration policies, and points instead to better alternatives such as enforcing banned-password lists. A great example is Azure AD password protection and multi-factor authentication. While we recommend these alternatives, they cannot be expressed or enforced with our recommended security configuration baselines, which are built on Windows' built-in

Group Policy settings and cannot include customer-specific values. This reinforces a larger important point about our baselines: while they are a solid foundation and should be part of your security strategy, they are not a complete security strategy.

"In this particular case, the small set of ancient password policies enforceable through Windows' security templates is not and cannot be a complete security strategy for user credential management. Removing a low-value setting from our baseline and not compensating with something else in the baseline does not mean we are lowering security standards. It simply reinforces that security cannot be achieved entirely with baselines."

"Why are we removing password-expiration policies?"

First, in order to avoid inevitable misunderstandings, we are talking here only about removing password-expiration policies. We do not propose changing requirements for minimum password length, history, or complexity.

Periodic password expiration is a defense only against the probability that a password, or hash, will be stolen during its validity interval and will be used by an unauthorized entity. If a password is never stolen, there's no need to expire it; and if you have evidence that a password has been stolen, you would presumably act immediately rather than wait for expiration to fix the problem.

With this being the case, users enjoy not having to change their passwords frequently; and it gives you the opportunity to include this service in your services offering.

Additional Food for Thought

Advise clients that they need to have policies in place to understand who, within their organization, has access to specific sites on the Internet. If you have someone in HR and they're using ADP, Paychex, Ceridian, or some other service, you must understand that this person has access to the company's financial information and/or HR. These services include, but are not limited to:

- E-mail services such as Office 365, Outlook.com, or a Google-hosted email.
- CRM software such as HubSpot, ZOHO, Salesforce, Infusionsoft, or Hootsuite.
- Travel services websites such as Expedia, Orbitz, American, Southwest, or any other airlines or travel booking services.
- E-commerce websites such as Amazon, Office Depot, Staples, or other office suppliers.
- Phone service providers such as your ISP, AT&T, BellSouth, T Mobile, Sprint, 8X8, or other VoIP services.
- Financial institutes such as PayPal, QuickBooks, any Banking websites, FreshBooks, or any credit processor sites.

Collaboration or data storage sites essentially anywhere that they would have file storage such as Box, Citrix File Share, Dropbox, OneDrive, SharePoint, Microsoft Teams, or any other services out there where you may have company data being stored and accessed by username and password. When you terminate an employee, IT needs to understand that they can't just change the active directory password, but they must also visit these file storage sites to change the passwords or remove the user access at that level. Maintain a list of these sites to ensure you're locking out the former employee. Consider an SOP, to be thorough with your security policies and add the necessary procedures when you need them.

Social media sites such as Facebook, LinkedIn, Twitter, Instagram, and anywhere else the user may have used the business e-mail address, as well as if the business uses these for business reasons, needs to be documented. If you give an employee access to social media, you need to ensure upon termination that you revoke that access. You need to understand the external threat that could be compromising data within your organization by simply terminating an employee or having their user name and password compromised or for sale on the dark web with no password policies in place to ensure that that password is changed frequently and a different password is used for every single site.

In addition to these, think about the number of sites that have actually been hacked in recent years, whether it was:

- LinkedIn, 2012, 117 million accounts
- Twitter, 32.8 million accounts
- Myspace, 2016, 360 million accounts (don't laugh, it still exists)
- Snap Chat, 4.6 million and employees spied on private messages…
- eBay, 145 million accounts

- Slack, 4 years after breach
- AOL, at least two elderly people (just seeing if you're reading)
- Adobe, 38 million accounts
- GameStop, stolen credit card data
- Orbitz, 880,000 cards compromised
- Yahoo over 500 million

The list goes on and on. If you've been to a health service provider such as Quest Diagnostics, Premera, Anthem, or Community Health Systems, all of these companies have recently had data breaches.

If you've shopped anywhere such as Lord & Taylor, Saks Fifth Avenue, Forever 21, Brooks Brothers, Neiman Marcus, Sally Beauty, Staples, Kmart, Albertsons, Target, or Home Depot. If you've eaten at P.F. Chang's, Chipotle, SONIC, or Arby's. If you've stayed at a location such as the Hilton, or most recently, the Marriott, which has had over 500 million users' data compromised. If you've used Uber for transportation. If you have utilized any of these services, your credit card and public identifiable information could have been stolen as well. There are many more such as Chase Manhattan Bank, as well as Equifax.

You need to take immediate steps to understand the dangers of having these sites compromised with your credentials and/or PII available for sale on the Dark Web. With this information available for sale out there, it is best to take measures to protect your credit and your identity by locking your credit at the three main credit bureaus.

I personally was a victim of the Equifax breach and have since locked my accounts. Any time I need to get utility services turned on for my rental property or a new property that I purchase, I turn the lock off temporarily while they verify my identity, or I have to show up in person with two forms of government ID. I would much rather go in person, or take the time to unlock my account, than leave my account open 24/7 for a hacker or would-be thief to compromise my identity and open accounts in my name, leaving a mess for me to have to clean up and prove it wasn't me.

By monitoring the dark web for my username and password as well as my clients', I know when a password is identified and I use this to educate my clients never to use that password, or any variation of that password, on any other sites, any time in the future. It's also an excellent time to have a conversation with your clients and educate them on password hygiene.

Outside of just monitoring for your passwords on the dark web, you should also have and understand a data breach response plan that is good for you, as well as for your clients. This book is not here to help you put a data breach response plan in place, but to encourage you to think about security as a primary, not a secondary thought.

Chapter 7

Common Sense Security And Basic Policies

Fortunately, simple security common sense within your MSP can help your engineers and staff keep you ahead of cybercriminals. As a first step, understand, read, and take a deep dive into Operation Cloud Hopper and make sure you understand how the Chinese government is trying to infiltrate managed service providers. Also, look at the things that engineers are overlooking today, such as remote desktop services and leaving RDP completely open for attack. A simple lockout password can help, but requiring two-factor authentication and/or VPN access in order to gain access to the remote desktop server is a best practice and should be followed closely.

You can no longer turn a blind eye to installing an FTP server or remote desktop server, thinking that a hacker won't find it online. These devices are being found within minutes of going live. Nor can you allow TOR browsers or rogue devices to be used to access your client's network. Let's look at some of the basic policies that every MSP should have in place.

Security policies must be signed by each staff member

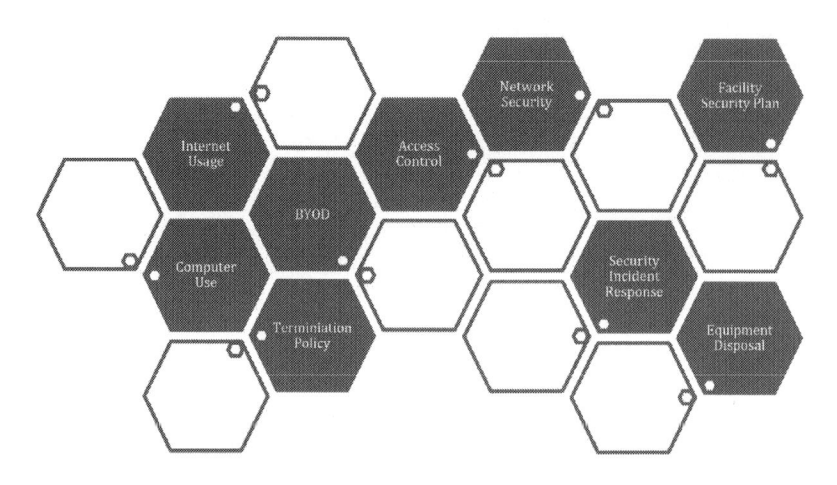

Security policies signed by each staff member

☐ **Bring Your Own Device (BYOD) policy:**

This policy will cover the devices that are allowed to access the MSP network, as well as clients' networks, either physically or through a VPN. Every device authorized must have your entire security stack deployed.

☐ **Computer Use Policy:**

This policy will cover what may be installed on the devices used to support your MSP and your clients. It should indicate what software is permitted and what is not allowed to be installed.

☐ **Internet Use Policy:**

This policy should cover what type of activity can be performed while using the device online, including the best practices in safe online searches and web browsing.

☐ **Access Control Policy:**

This policy assures that systems containing PII and/or sensitive company data are accessed only by those persons or software programs that have been granted appropriate access rights.

☐ **Network Security Policy:**

This policy describes the physical safeguards applicable for each server, desktop computer system, and wireless computer system used to access, transmit, receive, and store PII and sensitive company data to ensure that appropriate security is maintained. It also states which authorized employees have restricted access.

☐ **Security Incident Response:**

This policy is to help develop a plan for response and reporting of security incidents, including the identification of suspected or known incidents, the mitigation of the harmful effects of these incidents to the extent that is possible, and the documentation of security incidents and their outcomes. It tells your team who should receive incident reports as well.

☐ **Termination Policy:**

This policy should outline the necessary steps required to revoke both, physical and system access, to the Company's facilities, clients' networks and MSP's network resources.

☐ **Equipment Disposal:**

This policy outlines how the team will dispose of all media containing PII and sensitive company data, as well as the proper procedure to destroy the data and steps to ensure that no unauthorized access to the data takes place.

- ☐ **Facility Security Plan:**

This policy is to define the procedures of physical access to PII, sensitive company data, and the facilities in which each system will be housed while still ensuring that proper authorized access is allowed.

- ☐ **Written Information Security Policy:**

This policy creates effective administrative, technical, and physical safeguards for the protection of the PII of customers, clients, and employees, as well as sensitive company information that could be harmful if unauthorized access were to occur.

- ☐ **Sanction Policy:**

This policy governs employee sanctions and disciplinary actions from the company if an employee doesn't comply. All employees must comply with these policies and demonstrate competence in the requirements of all policies. This policy defines the important role and responsibilities of every employee.

Chapter 8

Steps To Better Protect Your MSP

Your family, clients, and employees are all depending on you to ensure that you can open for business tomorrow. That means taking all of the necessary steps to protect your MSP. Key steps include making sure that you have Dark Web research and monitoring. There should be mobile device management for employees' phones to ensure that if a phone is lost or stolen, or the employee is terminated, you can wipe the company data from that phone. Also, make sure you have encryption enabled on all devices that leave the office, as well as on laptops, tablets, and any device carrying the personal data of the business. Ensure that you have a firewall that offers data loss protection as well.

I recommend that you divide these separate services or tasks among your team and/or that you partner up with other MSPs you collaborate with and each come up with various service providers and vendors whom you've found helpful so that you may explore the pros and cons of each. In doing so, you'll be able to build and assemble your security stack, determine your cost and what your markup should be, assess what your market will bear, and decide how you will bundle this as a complete package that is inclusive of your managed services, as well as making a separate package for existing managed clients as an upsell security bundle.

Before you start, let's run through a checklist and ensure your MSP has been locked down!

☐ **Dark Web Monitoring:**

Enroll and ensure you receive alerts of Dark Web activity and monitoring for compromised passwords.

☐ **Vendor lockdown and passcode:**

Think ISP, cell phone carrier, managed print, other: You will want to ensure that you set up passcodes and/or pin codes with all providers that you use. Ask your finance person for a list of vendors you pay monthly, as well as annually.

☐ **SPAM filtering:**

Sign up and configure your e-mail to be filtered and flagged. Also, look for a company that reviews links within the message to ensure that the link is not malicious, or that there is a link to an infected payload.

☐ **Phishing e-mail:**

Send phishing e-mails to employees to ensure they don't fall for bogus e-mail links: You should do this randomly, yet as frequently as once a month.

☐ **E-mail encryption:**

Use e-mail encryption for secure message sending. Educate your employees, as well as clients, about the importance of NOT sending confidential information via insecure e-mail. Talk to your employees and ask them if they share passwords, PII, or

Client data via e-mail, and if so, educate them on why this is a bad idea. Just think, giving a hacker your username and password…

☐ **E-mail backup:**

Implement a third-party backup for Office 365. With the ability of hackers to encrypt e-mail today, you want to ensure you can restore from a backup in the unlikely event of a ransom attack.

☐ **Test restoration:**

Perform test restores of e-mails and files to ensure accurate backup procedures. Test, test, and retest before you have the need to depend on your backups.

☐ **SIEM:**

Ensure you deploy a SIEM that reports back to a third party SOC and leverage its team in the monitoring of network traffic.

☐ **Managed endpoint protection:**

Ensure that you are not using a legacy definition based AV. You will also want to make sure you're monitoring to ensure the AV is running the latest version of its software, so you can stay current and avoid new threats.

☐ **Managed breach detection:**

You may pick more than one provider for this service. We are seeing a lot of newcomers, and some are better than others. The threat landscape is changing, and so are the tools. Pick one (or two) and deploy them. Don't get hung up on, "What's next?"

☐ **RMM for updates and management:**

You should have a monthly to-do task to ensure all updates are current. Do not rely on this tool to do updates for you and hope that the automation works… Always check to ensure that a failure didn't occur before your competition finds out!

☐ **Wi-Fi policies:**

Wi-Fi passwords were changed internally, and only devices protected by advanced security solutions are allowed to connect to the company network. A guest network, featuring client isolation, is where all other devices, including staff smartphones, tablets, and all other non-protected devices not administered by corporate advanced security, can be allowed to connect. You should also have secured wireless access points, segregated networks from public and private browsing.

☐ **Enterprise level firewall:**

Edge protection should be at the top of your list and include DLP to ensure credit card and personally identifiable information is not leaving the network. Review all current firewall rules to ensure no inbound ports or RDP. VPN should be enabled for remote security browsing for all mobile devices to connect while away from the office.

☐ **Internal self-audit:**

Perform and run a self-audit to find out which employees are running their own devices versus company-owned devices. Ensure that BYOD devices are approved prior to techs using them to access a client's network.

☐ **Security Stack deployment:**

Install and verify that the complete security stack of protection is installed on EVERY device used to access company data and clients' networks. If a device is missing components of your new security stack, it should not be allowed to access clients' networks, much less yours.

☐ **Stack Audit:**

Ensure that all devices are cohesive with the security stack and that every tool has been installed at least once a quarter. Add a calendar reminder in Outlook to ensure that you don't forget to check all the machines.

☐ **Password manager:**

A password manager should be used to ensure every single password is unique and never used on more than one site or software. Additionally, make sure passwords do not follow a common phrase or term.

☐ **Account privileges escalation:**

Set up alerts for user accounts that have been promoted to admin privileges, monitoring, and alerting for the creation of new Admin users, along with alerts for user promotion to Admin. Chose a tool that is either real time or set to scan daily for changes.

☐ **Mobile device management:**

Install mobile device management software for every tablet and phone used within the organization. Ensure that you can wipe the device remotely in the event that it is stolen or lost.

☐ **Encryption:**

Encrypt all mobile devices to ensure that there is no breach if lost or stolen. Check your local laws. In Tennessee, if data is encrypted and a device is lost or stolen, it is NOT a data breach. If the device was NOT using encryption when lost or stolen, then it would be considered a breach and you would be mandated to report it to the government as well as to notify all clients.

☐ **Password lockout policy:**

Ensure that password lockout policies are configured on Active Directory from within Group Policy. Test to ensure that the account is locked after three failed attempts. This will help eliminate brute force attacks on your devices.

☐ **Business Continuity:**

Implement a business continuity service. Backups are one of the most important jobs of an IT professional, yet we see backup failures all the time within prospects' networks that we visit. Ensure that not only the backups are successful, but also that you can restore data from the backup.

☐ **Product lifecycle:**

Ensure that no end-of-life products are being used. All Windows XP, Windows 7, 2003 or 2008 servers, or older systems MUST be removed from your production environment ASAP... If you do not remove them, they must be in their own VLAN, or have the client sign a decline of service letter.

☐ **Insurance:**

I highly recommend you get coverage before you are wishing you had gotten coverage... Like I mentioned before, with the jewelry stores and doing due diligence, just because you have a policy does not ensure the insurance company will pay up… Make this a top priority to get handled by the end of the day!

- ☐ **Default password policy:**

Change default passwords on all devices including switches, cameras, IOT devices, and make sure no open ports enable inbound traffic to said devices. The recommendation is that your primary network should not contain any IOT type devices. Segregate them out on VLANs if needed.

- ☐ **LAN permitted device policy:**

Ensure the removal of all devices such as Alexa, Nest, Google Home, smart TVs, smart refrigerators, and any other devices that are network-enabled from the network infrastructure (LAN).

Chapter 9

Enable Multi Factor Authentication on EVERY Login, EVERY Portal

Two-factor authentication is critical to have on all logins that we use, especially the ones that allow us to access our clients. 2FA, or multi-factor, offers an extra layer of protection besides just passwords. It's harder for cybercriminals to get the second authentication factor. They would have to manipulate/spoof your phone number, if you are using texting, or would have to get access to your 2FA apps. This drastically reduces the chance for hackers to succeed. In one MSP's case, the Administrator's password was the same for his Google account, which he was using for 2FA. I'll repeat what I said previously: never use the same password twice or on more than one site/service!

A few examples of two-factor authentication methods that you most likely are already using:

- The token issued by your bank, which generates a specific code at a specific time. You use it with your username and password for Internet banking.

- A one-time password that you receive as a text message on your mobile phone. You use it when you want to log into your various accounts.
- A one-time password that you receive as a phone message on your mobile or office phone.
- A random password generated by an app like Google Authenticator or Authy. You use it to log into your e-mail or online portals.

I have created a checklist for you to follow, and ensure that you have 2FA enabled on everything that you possibly could implement it on… This list may not be complete, and you should always make your own list of sites and services to ensure you don't leave any site unprotected. Again, this is a necessary step to help in protecting your MSP from hackers. Warning: This takes a lot of time and effort. Take it slow but continue to work on it daily until completion. Use the space below each checklist item for notes.

☐ **Remote monitoring and management (RMM)**

_____
_____
_____
_____

☐ **Professional services automation (PSA)**

_____
_____
_____
_____

Enable Multi Factor Authentication on EVERY Login, EVERY Portal

- ☐ **Office 365 portal**

_____
_____
_____
_____

- ☐ **Office 365 e-mail and One Drive online applications and logins:**

_____
_____
_____
_____

- ☐ **SPAM filtering enabled and blocking**

_____
_____
_____
_____

- ☐ **SPAM filter/provider both to access SPAM and to management portal:**

_____
_____
_____
_____

☐ **DNS Host**

_____

_____

_____

_____

☐ **Remote access platform(s)**

_____

_____

_____

_____

☐ **Domain hosting provider**

_____

_____

_____

_____

☐ **Website host provider**

_____

_____

_____

_____

Enable Multi Factor Authentication on EVERY Login, EVERY Portal

- [ ] **Accounting portal**

- [ ] **Cloud vendor(s)**

- [ ] **VoIP admin portal**

- [ ] **Dark Web provider**

- ☐ **Phishing test provider**

_____
_____
_____
_____

- ☐ **DNS filter portal**

_____
_____
_____
_____

- ☐ **Managed breach detection portal**

_____
_____
_____
_____

Managed end point protection/antivirus

_____
_____
_____
_____

Enable Multi Factor Authentication on EVERY Login, EVERY Portal

☐ **Cloud controller for Wi-Fi**

☐ **Hosted switch controller**

☐ **Management software for management of networking and power devices**

☐ **Business continuity and backup disaster recovery portal**

- [ ] **Online file-only backups**

- [ ] **Firewall partner portals**

- [ ] **Client network documentation portal**

- [ ] **Instant messaging apps**

Enable Multi Factor Authentication on EVERY Login, EVERY Portal

☐ **Network security monitoring tool(s)**

___

☐ **Network scanning tools**

___

☐ **Online file storage, sharing, sync providers**

___

☐ **Password management tools**

- [ ] **Infrastructure monitoring**

_____
_____
_____
_____

- [ ] **Online policy management**

_____
_____
_____
_____

- [ ] **CIO management software**

_____
_____
_____
_____

- [ ] **Process for non-MFA applications and websites**

_____
_____
_____
_____

Enable Multi Factor Authentication on EVERY Login, EVERY Portal

☐ **Other:**

_____
_____
_____
_____

☐ **Other:**

_____
_____
_____
_____

Chapter 10

Factoring In Other Security Concerns

Are you STILL using generic dictionary passwords?

Passwords are plagued with problems and vulnerabilities that make them inadequate for many of the authentication roles in which they are used. Consequentially, simple passwords are falling out of favor. Security professionals are pushing for multi-factor authentication in order to compensate for password shortcomings.

What makes passwords so bad? They tend to be easily compromised. Why are they easy to compromise? Because the use of weak passwords, blank passwords, default passwords, improper password storage, and insufficient IT controls allow easy passwords to be acceptable.

Guessable passwords are password choices that are obvious or able to be guessed by other people. These are usually things like kids' names, pet names, kids' birthdates, favorite sports team, and/or dictionary words. These are easy for users to remember, but because of that, they are also easy for unauthorized users to determine.

We recently had a training class here at our office, and everyone chose a password. We ran a password cracking software against the passwords used and found that all but one was guessed within an hour. Let's review some checklist items that you need to ensure you have in place to protect your MSP.

Consider all the passwords that have been obtained during previous data breaches mentioned earlier in this book. Over a billion passwords are in clear text and can be used to try and guess their way into systems. Below are some instances that you should consider reviewing and correcting.

☐ **All standard admin passwords for firewalls and servers have been reset with longer and more complex passwords. This is for internal servers and firewalls. Every client must have different passwords!**

_____

_____

_____

_____

☐ **Process for non-MFA applications and websites**

_____

_____

_____

_____

Factoring In Other Security Concerns

- ☐ Social media password lockdown and alerts configured (Additionally, who should receive the login alerts?)

_____
_____
_____

- ☐ What social media accounts does your business use? List all that apply.

_____
_____
_____

Who is an admin of each social media platform?

_____
_____
_____
_____

- ☐ Know who has access to website as an admin

_____
_____
_____
_____

☐ **Set a password notification policy to ensure you are notified of all logins to Gmail, Facebook, LinkedIn, etc.**

_____

_____

_____

☐ **Ensure all passwords are configured in the password manager for quick deactivation**

_____

_____

_____

☐ **Put Office 365 on lockdown!**

(Login to dashboard Administrator contact email. https://securescore.office.com/#!/dashboard

The average score for most companies with no security enhancements is 37. You should lockdown Office 365 to achieve the highest possible score. (Additionally, you should use this in your new client acquisition process, as well as run it on all of your existing clients. This tool alone can generate countless revenue if used properly, as well as keep the competition from using it against you.)

My starting score is _____

Factoring In Other Security Concerns

☐ **Ensure no sharing of passwords across clients' devices and network infrastructure**

☐ **Vendors such as ISP, cell phone provider, VoIP, Ingram and Dell have PINs or passwords for making changes to account information: ensure all pins are unique and documented. It is recommended to use a password manager to keep up with these security codes and pins**

Chapter 11

Why Partnering With An MSSP Is Necessary

The title of this book is a play on words, and as far as the majority of MSP's are concerned, we will never become a true MSSP. Not because we don't want to, but more so because of what is involved with creating such a service. My approach is to ensure that MSPs are becoming "security-centric" and starting to think more about security, and not just pro-active managed services. I was fortunate enough to travel to Toronto a couple of years back and was able to tour a true MSSP. This MSSP, at the time, was doing over $250M in annual revenue and their competition is IBM. Now, when I say I got to "tour" the facility, there are a couple of things that you have to understand. People on the tour didn't get to actually go inside the SOC (security operations center,) but view it through a bulletproof pane of glass. When the tour started, and we walked up to the area, we had a view of a full wall of TVs monitoring threats. As well as looking through, we could also see Engineers scrolling through data on their screens. As soon as an Engineer saw us, the glass went cloudy and killed the view. Later they cleared the smokescreen windows and allowed us to see their Engineers, monitoring systems and doing what they do best. In observation, the entry to the SOC room was a one-way turnstile that was activated with a keycard. Once past the turnstile, there was a door that was operated by a biometric scanner to authorize the person. If the person couldn't be verified, they would be stuck and await a security escort out of the building, or to authorities. This multifactor approach to entering into the SOC securely, as well as the equipment and buildout, would alone keep a smaller MSP from being able to afford the costs to start building out a true SOC. When considering if you should become an MSSP and build a SOC versus outsourcing, remember back to the first few years "Cloud" computing became a hot topic. We watched countless companies try to build out cloud infrastructure on their own. We even watched as multiple MSP's partnered together to start a cloud platform, and as some have been successful, some have closed and even gave users 30 days to move. Lots of capital had to be laid out, and even at the turn of a profit, much of that equipment was starting to get outdated. Not telling you that you won't be successful, just sharing that we should learn from history.

If you are focused on growing your business and serving customers, it will be hard to focus simultaneously on all of the security triggers that are happening throughout the day as well. Partnering with an MSSP will give you an added layer of security and free you to do the work you do best. At a true MSSP, the SOC will monitor alerts from your threat-monitoring platform(s), your breach detection system, your endpoint protection, and your firewall alerts, bringing you substantial resources and access to well-trained engineers. They are masters at eliminating the noise and reading the alerts that matter most. It's like reading the lines of code in the Matrix... By partnering with a true MSSP, who has a SOC and allows your vendor agnostic devices to report back to them, you will have great peace of mind, knowing that alerts are being monitored 24/7.

Let's take a look at a few of the benefits of partnering with an MSSP. We will look at the specific ways that they can help you to build out and deliver your security stack with confidence.

- **Extension of your team:**

    Even if you have Engineers on your team that are security-focused and intelligent, you wouldn't want to have them sitting and monitoring alerts 24/7. By having an extended team watching over all of the alerts from your client's devices, as well as yours, you will have a vital resource in times of need. Let's say that the SOC identifies a threat. They will engage with your team and work together to eradicate the identified problem. Because these folks work with monitoring and removing threats all day every day, they are well versed in how to handle a situation. If you had a breach today, would your staff know the proper procedures to ensure minimum damage and not be adding to the liability of the damages? By allowing the SOC to focus on security monitoring, you allow your team to focus on what they do well.

- **Threat intelligence and education:**

    By partnering with the right MSSP, you are relying on them to protect your client's networks. These SOCs typically have highly trained engineers who are always working to improve their skill sets and are constantly learning what new threats are being identified. With the speed of new attacks, including zero-day, it is best to partner with a company whose focus is 100% on security and threat response. Most MSPs don't enforce simple Microsoft, nor CompTIA, much less high-end security training.

- **24/7 security monitoring:**

    You will have confidence and peace of mind knowing that the SOC is watching over all of your networks, even while you sleep. By having a team combing through and reacting to malicious activity, you can focus on business growth, vacations, or whatever your focus is, all while being able to rest easy knowing that if a breach or threat occurs, the partner will spring into action to limit or eliminate any damage to your client's information.

- **Lower Costs**

    We've already mentioned the cost of building out a SOC. Now, think about how many engineers are required to provide 24/7 support and what those salaries might look like. This alone could be into the hundreds of thousands of dollars, not to mention the ongoing training and maintenance of the SOC. The cost to enable multiple vendors to feed into the SOC infrastructure, as well as the cross-training on various platforms, causes costs to skyrocket quickly. By partnering with an MSSP who has multiple clients and multiple engineers, the cost per partner gets lower and more affordable.

- **Compliance and standardization:**

    It doesn't matter which compliance standard your client is mandated to comply with; the MSSP can help you to ensure that the client stays within compliance. You can depend on your MSSP for recommendations, as well as they can help you with reports and audits. Have you ever had a client going through a third-party audit, or penetration testing, and have a questionnaire that goes on for days asking about how reporting is done, threats are identified, as well as how often systems are scanned or updated? Let the MSSP assist you in answering those and many more audit questions, as well as helping to define RTO (recovery time objectives) and other key factors in compliance handling.

Choosing an MSSP To Partner with Your MSP

MSPs are not created equal, and the same is true for MSSPs. Research needs to be done to ensure that you know exactly the right partner to help you protect your clients from the hackers and scammers. A few things to look for are:

- What certifications do the engineers hold, and when was the last time they were updated?
- How do they hire and screen new engineers?
- What are the qualifications of new engineers, and what are the onboarding and training programs offered?
- Are they all located within your own country?
- How many years of experience does each have, as well as years of combined experience?

- What services do they offer, and what vendors are recommended/required?
- Is their SOC monitored and staffed 24/7?
- What is their complete list of services offered?
- What is their contractual agreement and its length?
- What compliance standards do you support?
- How do they communicate with your team members?
- What types of reports will be provided to the MSP, as well as client-facing?
- Do they offer MDR (managed detection and response)?
- Do you assist with RISK assessments?
- Do they provide real time monitoring of all systems?
- How do they handle ticket workflows and escalations?
- Will our team have any visibility into the SOC for reporting or monitoring purposes? How long has their company been in business?
- Do they have references that we can talk too? Another MSP preferably.
- How are you different than other MSSPs?
- How will you integrate with our ticketing system, and how do they handle false positives?

Working with an MSSP goes beyond just hiring a third-party team to help protect your clients. Look at them as a business partner that is an extension of your team and talk to other MSP's who are their partners, as well as speak to a couple of their engineers to get a pulse on how well they love the company and what the culture is like. Speaking to engineers is a great way to ensure that you are partnering with someone who you will value and trust as you both move forward in the partnership. Do your due diligence to ensure that you know who you are hiring and exactly where the hand-off is before there is a breach or security event!

Chapter 12

Third Party Validation

It is highly recommended that your clients have a security audit, penetration testing at least once every 2-3 years, depending on hardware refresh cycles. This audit should be done by an outside vendor. Working with this vendor will allow you to review the results so that you can remediate and take care of any issues that may have arisen. Cybercriminal activity and regulatory compliance requirements create a demand for effective risk management and security controls. To ensure that MSPs have securely locked down their own networks, as well as clients', it is recommended that each network gets a third-party validation and that ensure engineers didn't leave any vulnerabilities open.

- **Assessment:**

    A security and compliance assessment is a process in which the third-party will interview employees, examine systems, and review the network framework to look for weaknesses and gaps in security. This assessment should give you a baseline from which you can improve upon the security weaknesses identified. Additionally, you will discover what you should be focused on. Then proper measures should be made to ensure that your network is as secure as possible. One major thing to consider is that no matter how secure or clean your assessment is, you should not stop taking action to ensure that gaps don't get created after the fact. You should always be focused on keeping the network secure.

- **Risk Management:**

    Risk management is taking action on the findings of a security assessment. This is typically done when identified threats and risks are determined, as well as the likelihood of the risk impacting your business. Work with the third-party vendor and your team to work through the prioritization of your findings based on the risks.

- **Remediation:**

    When a risk is found, remediation steps will need to be taken, whether through the implementation of new security controls or via modification of existing controls, ensuring each risk is mitigated by fixing the risk. Each risk will need to be reviewed once the new steps or measures are in place to ensure the network is secured. New policies may need to be created, firewall rules changed, or even a firewall replacement might be required. Documentation should also be updated on how to handle arising situations.

- **Penetration testing:**

    It is critical and, in some cases, mandated that the companies get a penetration test. During the test, you will typically work with an ethical hacker, and you might even receive a device to connect to your LAN. The test will look for any vulnerabilities that can be used to compromise your network security. A series of attacks will be performed over a period of time, typically a week, and the ethical hacker will use tools to compromise controls within the infrastructure, including IOT (Internet of things) devices. Upon completion, you should receive a report to notify you of the findings and what would be required for remediation.

Third-party validation of your security is great for companies wanting to ensure that they are compliant, as well as those who simply want to protect the business they have built and grown. The benefits will also come into play in the event of a breach and an insurance claim would need to be filed. By showing that you've taken steps to secure your network, you are following the best practices and doing your due diligence to protect your business, your data, as well as your clients' data, and systems.

Chapter 13

New Security Breach Notification Laws: What You Need to Know

It's Monday morning and one of your employees notifies you that they lost their laptop at a Starbucks over the weekend, apologizing profusely. Aside from the cost and inconvenience of buying a new laptop, could you be on the hook for bigger costs? And should you notify all of your clients?

Maybe, depending on where you live and what type of data you had stored on that laptop. Forty-six of the 50 states, plus Washington D.C., Guam, Puerto Rico, and the Virgin Islands, have security-breach laws outlining what businesses must do if they expose any kind of client or employee personal information. Practically every single business is directly affected by these laws. (Currently, the only states without such laws are Alabama, Kentucky, New Mexico, and South Dakota, but that is likely to change.) Check with your local government to understand what is considered a breach and the steps to take in the event of one.

An Emerging Trend in Business Law

Because companies are storing more and more data on their employees and clients, states are starting to aggressively enforce data breach and security laws that lay out the responsibilities for businesses on capturing and storing personal data.

What do most states consider confidential or sensitive data? Definitely medical and financial records, such as credit card numbers, credit scores, and bank account numbers, but also addresses, phone numbers, social security numbers, birthdays, and in some cases, even purchase history—information that almost every single company normally keeps on its clients.

"We Did Our Best" Is No Longer An Acceptable Answer

With millions of cybercriminals working daily to hack systems, and with employees accessing more and more confidential client data, there is no known way to absolutely, positively guarantee that you won't have a data breach. However, your efforts to put in place good, solid best practices in security will go a long way to help you avoid hefty fines. The definition of "reasonable security" is constantly evolving, but here are some basic things to consider in order to avoid being labeled irresponsible:

1. **Managing access:**

    Who can access the confidential information you store in your business? Is this information easily accessible by everyone in your company? What is your policy on taking data out of the office via mobile devices?

2. **IT security and passwords:**

    The more sensitive the data, the higher the level of security you need to keep on it. Are your passwords easy to crack? Is the data encrypted? Secured behind a strong firewall? If not, why?

3. **Training:**

    One of the biggest causes for data breaches is the human element: employees who accidentally download viruses and malware that allow hackers easy access. Do you have a data security policy? A password policy? Do you have training to help employees understand how to use e-mail and the Internet responsibly?

4. **Physical security:**

    It has become increasingly more common for thieves to break into offices, stealing servers, laptops, and other digital devices. Additionally, paper contracts and other physical documents containing sensitive information should be locked up or scanned and encrypted.

The bottom line is this:

Data security is something that EVERY business is now responsible for, and not addressing this important issue has consequences that go far beyond the legal aspect; it can seriously harm your reputation with clients! Be smart about this. Talk to your attorney about your legal responsibility.

Chapter 14

Complying with Compliance

Compliance, regulation basics, penalties and fines, GDPR, the right to be forgotten to minimize your liability, all of the legal jargon, and thousands upon thousands of lines of compliance can be overwhelming. Can you become compliant? With state and federal governments having two sets of information that don't align, do you or don't you destroy the data? Can we help our clients and ensure that they remain compliant?

The quick answer is yes: compliance is obtainable! Neither your network infrastructure, nor a cloud solution, nor anything we open out of the box and attach to our current IT solution, is or was compliant straight out of the gate. Compliance is attainable by having a third-party company run a scan on your traditional or Cloud network infrastructure to see what is not meeting the minimal requirements. These reports will tell you what modifications need to take place in order for you to be compliant. We must assist clients in assuring their information meets these standards.

Additionally, e-mail can be archived and searchable. With each solution, you have different needs and requests. Having e-mail available, searchable, and archived is a feature required for certain financial institutions' compliances and is also obtainable.

Compliance can also be ensured in either environment by putting policies and procedures into place. Using a policy manager, you can set passwords to require a certain number of letters and characters, set passwords to expire every x number of days, and user groups for security purposes and ensuring that the correct employees have access and others don't. There are countless policies that can be enabled.

The Federal Information Security Management Act (FISMA) of 2002 has become the basis for most data compliance standards within the USA. Understanding FISMA's "Triad" lets you and your client understand the goals of whatever compliance they fall into. Keeping this in simple terms with our clients, we can use The Triad, or acronym CIA as:

- Confidentiality– preserving authorized restrictions on access and disclosure, which includes means for protecting personal privacy and confidential data
- Integrity– guarding against improper data modification or destruction and ensuring data accuracy and authenticity
- Availability– ensuring timely and reliable access to the confidential data

The goal here is to focus on and protect the data! And in order to do that, we have to enable the safeguards. The best way to enable safeguards is to understand the C.I.A. concept. Here we can look at how this applies to daily corporate structure and use. The safeguards, or controls, are designed to look at an organization holistically from three primary aspects:

- Technical– the technology, and its policies and procedures for its use, that are in place to defend confidential data as well as to control access to it.
- Physical– the physical measures, as well as the policies and procedures, used to protect confidential data from unauthorized physical access and also protection from natural and environmental hazards.
- Administrative– the maintenance, policies, and procedures with regards to the security measures that protect confidential data.

It is a common misconception that the above are used ONLY for HIPAA! By knocking out 95% of the IT framework following NIST, and by understanding the concept of data security via C.I.A. while combining the practical knowledge of how to safeguard it, we can now build the framework! The most universally used cybersecurity framework is NIST. NIST, while US-based, is accepted worldwide by corporations and other governments as a model for cyber defense. Other major frameworks, such as PCI, DSS, ISO, and CIS, are at least partially or fully based on NIST's fundamentals. The following are the Five Functions of NIST.

NIST Function: Identify:

- Identify physical and software assets to establish asset management.

- Identify the business environment the organization supports, including its role in the supply chain and its place in the critical infrastructure sector.
- Identify cybersecurity policies, legal requirements, and regulatory requirements to define a Governance program for cybersecurity.
- Identify current vulnerabilities, threats (internal and external), as well as risk response measures in order to create a risk assessment model.
- Identify and create a risk management strategy, including risk tolerances.
- Identify and create a supply chain risk management strategy, including priorities for defense, constraints based on position in the supply chain, and its risks.

NIST FUNCTION: Protect

- Create protections for identity management and access control for both physical and remote access.
- Create awareness and training programs, including role based and privileged user training.
- Create a data security protection solution consistent with the risk strategy to protect the C.I.A. of confidential information.
- Create processes and procedures to maintain and manage the protection of the systems and assets.
- Protect the organization through maintenance activities, including remote assets.

- Manage the technology used to create a cyber defense strategy.

NIST FUNCTION: Detect

- Ensure that anomalies and events are detected, and their potential impact is understood.
- Implement continuous security monitoring to discover cyber threats and verify the effectiveness of protective measures, including network and physical activities.
- Maintain detection processes to have a constant awareness of anomalous events.

NIST FUNCTION: Respond

- Ensure that response planning processes are adhered to during and after an incident.
- Manage communication during and after the event with the organization, law enforcement, and other stakeholders.
- Conduct analysis to ensure effective response and support recovery activities, including forensics, to determine the impact of the event.
- Perform mitigation activities to prevent the expansion of an event and to resolve the incident.
- Implement Improvements to the cyber defense strategy based on lessons learned from the incident.

NIST FUNCTION: Recover

- Ensure that the organization implements recovery planning processes and procedures to restore assets and operations back to normal.
- Implement improvements based on lessons learned and reviews of existing strategies.
- Ensure that internal and external communications are coordinated and completed to alert all to return to normal operations.
-

FOUNDATIONAL TECHNOLOGY: The critical components for cyber defense

- Next Generation Firewalls
- Next Generation Antivirus
- Enterprise Level switches and wireless access points
- 24/7 SIEM/SOC Monitoring for all of the above
- Encryption systems (at rest and in transit)
- Awareness and training programs: what this doesn't cover is everything beyond the technical solution such as asset management, policies, processes, etc.

So, where do you go from here? Considerations that must be dealt with:

- The 5% of compliance that isn't covered here.
- Making the right choices in cyber defense technology
- Never standing still (This is a serious MSP issue!)

Understand where your limitations are, as not everyone should be doing compliance work! Building alliances through colleagues, such as joining organizations or online groups, are great for this. You need to ask yourself if compliance is something that you want to invest your time and your team's time in. Or, partner with a third-party that focuses on that as a primary business model.

Chapter 15

Going to Market

I highly recommend, as you're taking this journey, that you write blog articles and/or do LinkedIn videos, and even Facebook Live, to educate and better articulate the services that you're looking at and what you're building within your organization. Posting these blogs, and/or being featured in an article by one of your vendors, is a good way to build credibility. It will also have your clients engaging and asking better questions.

Another way to build credibility is to host webinars and seminars. I highly recommend that you do technical business reviews with your clients. As you're talking with them, let them know that you're working on an evolving security stack. I, personally, did this over coffee and breakfast while meeting with my clients outside of their office and let them know that the old managed services model we had sold them years ago was no longer everything they needed to protect their network. We explained that we needed additional tools and security measures put in place, and that these would come at a cost. The security landscape is constantly changing and evolving, and we need to constantly evaluate tools to better protect ourselves as well, as our clients, from these growing threats. Once we built out and tested our security stack, we explained, we would be taking these to market and coming to the clients to ensure that we kept our costs low, given that they had been long-time loyal clients to us.

When you have conversations like this, you'll also want to have your decline of service letter, found in the back of this book, as well as your master service agreements renewed. You'll need to hire an attorney for this one, and make sure that you work on the art of closing the sale through storytelling. People don't like to be sold; they like to be educated so they can make an informed decision on what they should make a purchase, and why. Through sharing stories of data breaches, security incidents, and how companies could have prevented these events by having security as a focus and outsourcing to a professional, they can be avoided. Share stories of wire fraud instances, as well as how scammers get employees to purchase iTunes gift cards, and how simple education could prevent these scams and loss of money. One such thing you can share is any company working with wire transfers is to enable a simple policy. When wiring instructions are sent, leave out 3-5 digits of the account or routing number. Have the party wiring the money simply call to get the missing numbers. They should verify they have everything, and this verification can prevent money from being sent to hackers or scammers.

I was having a discussion with an old break/fix client just last week that didn't want to spend $40,000 a year because they had to replace seven machines due to a virus outbreak. "How much is it to just replace these machines, fix our network, and not have to deal with the hackers?" he said. "I'm not paying you $40,000 because I've never had to pay that before."

I had to use storytelling and explain that network security today is not comparable to what service you've paid for in the past. (Or haven't paid for.) No longer can we turn a blind eye to having hackers infiltrate our systems and using our computers for malicious purposes. When the FBI determines which IP address and which computers are being used, they're not going to show up at the hacker's door. They're going to show up at the door of your client.

We had a client with an International truck that they would use for deliveries. One day the Police came by with video surveillance of the company truck being used and driven by a criminal to do a smash and grab at a convenience store that was closed. A criminal was "borrowing" their truck on the weekend while the business was closed to back into and bust through the front of a convenience store. They would fill the truck with alcohol, lottery tickets, cigarettes, tobacco, anything of value, and then drive off. The police suspected that they then would, then, store the contents at a remote location and deliver the truck back to the client's site prior to Monday morning when the company opened for business.

The client had no idea, for months on end, that their truck was being used for malicious purposes and breaking into convenience stores, until the authorities showed up in their office with video surveillance showing the truck, inclusive of their logo.

Furthermore, we've had clients that have had their systems compromised in years past, and the activity that we saw on the machines was a remote user deploying the machine to make purchases with stolen credit cards. Had the authorities been notified of the IP address of the victim or the computer performing these crimes, they would have shown up at our client's doorstep.

We need to go to market, have a conversation with our clients, and educate them on the dangers of what's out there. We've also got to teach them what the tools we are building in our security stack do and how these tools can better protect them and ensure, if there is a cyber-attack, that their cyber insurance company will not decline their claim.

Cybersecurity Self-Assessment

Organizations are faced with significant challenges when attempting to secure their digital assets from an onslaught of increasingly sophisticated and effective cyber threats and attacks. In addition, Federal and State governments continue to produce new regulations that require organizations to build comprehensive cybersecurity programs and take responsibility for protecting themselves and others from various threats and vulnerabilities.

When presented with the new responsibility of creating and implementing effective cybersecurity programs, executives of organizations can quickly become overwhelmed.

This Cybersecurity Self-Assessment is designed to provide insight to those responsible for achieving regulatory compliance and protecting assets. The assessment is a high-level evaluation that will help determine the cybersecurity preparedness level of the organization based on the widely adopted NIST (National Institute of Standards and Technology) Cybersecurity Framework.

The NIST Cybersecurity Framework requires adopters to:

(1) Have the capability to **Identify** cyber threats and vulnerabilities,

(2) **Protect** themselves accordingly with security controls and defenses,

(3) Have the capability to **Detect** if security controls have been compromised,

(4) **Respond** to cyber-attacks, incidents and breaches and lastly,

(5) **Recover** from cyber-attacks, incidents, and breaches.

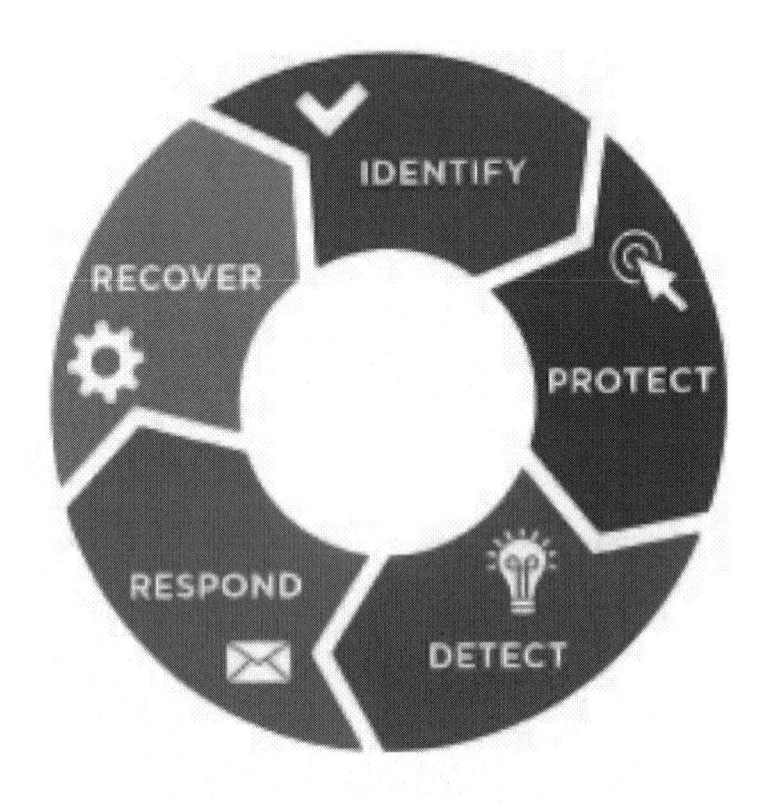

The assessment is segmented into five Sections: Identify, Protect, Detect, Respond, and Recover. Each section contains several statements. Read each statement carefully and then assign a numeric value using the assessment scale below. The numeric value assigned to the statement should be most representative of your organization's current capability or status.

Numeric Value	Statement Compliance
1	Disagree
2	Somewhat Disagree
3	Somewhat Agree
4	Agree

After assigning a numeric value to all statements for a section, add all numeric values for a section total and refer to the results recommendation section.

Section 1: Identify

1. All physical systems and devices within the organization are inventoried.

    (1) Disagree

    (2) Somewhat Disagree

    (3) Somewhat Agree

    (4) Agree

2. All software platforms and applications within the organization are inventoried.

    (1) Disagree

    (2) Somewhat Disagree

    (3) Somewhat Agree

    (4) Agree

3. All systems, devices, software platforms, and applications are classified and prioritized based on their criticality and business value.

    (1) Disagree

    (2) Somewhat Disagree

    (3) Somewhat Agree

    (4) Agree

4. The organization has clearly defined cybersecurity roles and responsibilities for internal users, external vendors, customers, and partners.

    (1) Disagree

    (2) Somewhat Disagree

(3) Somewhat Agree
   (4) Agree

5. **The organization has written information security policies and procedures.**
   (1) Disagree
   (2) Somewhat Disagree
   (3) Somewhat Agree
   (4) Agree

6. **The organization clearly understands all legal and regulatory requirements regarding cybersecurity.**
   (1) Disagree
   (2) Somewhat Disagree
   (3) Somewhat Agree
   (4) Agree

7. **Cybersecurity risks are identified and managed by a governance and risk management process.**
   (1) Disagree
   (2) Somewhat Disagree
   (3) Somewhat Agree
   (4) Agree

8. **Cybersecurity risk tolerance is determined, expressed in policy, and agreed upon by all stakeholders.**
   (1) Disagree
   (2) Somewhat Disagree
   (3) Somewhat Agree
   (4) Agree

Section 2: Protect

1. **A security awareness training program is in place, and all users are provided training at least annually.**
   (1) Disagree
   (2) Somewhat Disagree
   (3) Somewhat Agree
   (4) Agree

2. **Critical or sensitive data is protected by encryption technology at rest and in transit.**
   (1) Disagree
   (2) Somewhat Disagree
   (3) Somewhat Agree
   (4) Agree

3. **Network segmentation is used logically or physically to separate systems according to policy.**
   (1) Disagree
   (2) Somewhat Disagree
   (3) Somewhat Agree
   (4) Agree

4. **The organization has a formal change of management process.**
   (1) Disagree
   (2) Somewhat Disagree
   (3) Somewhat Agree
   (4) Agree

5. There is a formal process documented for conducting, maintaining, and testing data backups.
   (1) Disagree
   (2) Somewhat Disagree
   (3) Somewhat Agree
   (4) Agree

6. Data backups of critical systems have at least three copies, two of which are located on different media, and at least one of which is physically situated offsite.
   (1) Disagree
   (2) Somewhat Disagree
   (3) Somewhat Agree
   (4) Agree

7. All systems are secured and hardened using industry best practices or according to policy.
   (1) Disagree
   (2) Somewhat Disagree
   (3) Somewhat Agree
   (4) Agree

8. There is a formal vulnerability and patch management program in which systems, devices, software, and applications are regularly scanned for known vulnerabilities and then patched or upgraded accordingly.
   (1) Disagree
   (2) Somewhat Disagree
   (3) Somewhat Agree
   (4) Agree

9. Access permissions and authorizations are managed, incorporating the principles of least privilege and separation of duties.

   (1) Disagree

   (2) Somewhat Disagree

   (3) Somewhat Agree

   (4) Agree

10. Physical access to critical systems and devices is managed.

    (1) Disagree

    (2) Somewhat Disagree

    (3) Somewhat Agree

    (4) Agree

11. Multi-factor authentication is used to authenticate critical systems or applications.

    (1) Disagree

    (2) Somewhat Disagree

    (3) Somewhat Agree

    (4) Agree

12. There is a formal, written disaster recovery (DR) and business continuity plan (BCP).

    (1) Disagree

    (2) Somewhat Disagree

    (3) Somewhat Agree

    (4) Agree

13. **There is a formal, written incident response and recovery plan.**
    (1) Disagree
    (2) Somewhat Disagree
    (3) Somewhat Agree
    (4) Agree

14. **Perimeter defenses such as firewalls and intrusion detection/prevention systems are implemented and managed.**
    (1) Disagree
    (2) Somewhat Disagree
    (3) Somewhat Agree
    (4) Agree

15. **Endpoint protection, such as anti-virus and anti-malware defenses, are implemented and managed.**
    (1) Disagree
    (2) Somewhat Disagree
    (3) Somewhat Agree
    (4) Agree

Section 3: Detect

1. The organization has a clear definition of normal network operations and expected data flows for users and systems.
   (1) Disagree
   (2) Somewhat Disagree
   (3) Somewhat Agree
   (4) Agree

2. The organization has the capability to collect and correlate events and logs from multiple sources, systems, devices, or applications.
   (1) Disagree
   (2) Somewhat Disagree
   (3) Somewhat Agree
   (4) Agree

3. The network, physical environment, and user activity are actively monitored to detect potential cybersecurity events.
   (1) Disagree
   (2) Somewhat Disagree
   (3) Somewhat Agree
   (4) Agree

4. The organization always knows when a security control has been comprised.
   (1) Disagree
   (2) Somewhat Disagree
   (3) Somewhat Agree
   (4) Agree

Section 4: Response

1. Roles and responsibilities for incident response personnel are thoroughly defined and communicated.
   (1) Disagree
   (2) Somewhat Disagree
   (3) Somewhat Agree
   (4) Agree

2. Cybersecurity incidents are properly communicated throughout the organization when they occur. Information related to the event is shared in a manner consistent with the incident response plan.
   (1) Disagree
   (2) Somewhat Disagree
   (3) Somewhat Agree
   (4) Agree

3. Formal, documented processes and procedures for investigating notifications of suspicious activity are executed and maintained by the incident response team.
   (1) Disagree
   (2) Somewhat Disagree
   (3) Somewhat Agree
   (4) Agree

4. Formal, documented processes and procedures exist to ensure the preservation of forensic evidence during or after an event.
   (1) Disagree
   (2) Somewhat Disagree

(3) Somewhat Agree
   (4) Agree
5. **The organization has the capability to quickly contain and mitigate cybersecurity incidents.**
   (1) Disagree
   (2) Somewhat Disagree
   (3) Somewhat Agree
   (4) Agree
6. **The incident response plan is regularly reviewed and updated based on test results or actual events.**
   (1) Disagree
   (2) Somewhat Disagree
   (3) Somewhat Agree
   (4) Agree

Section 5: Recover

1. The disaster recovery (DR) and business continuity plan (BCP) is tested regularly, and at least annually.

    (1) Disagree

    (2) Somewhat Disagree

    (3) Somewhat Agree

    (4) Agree

2. The organization is capable of recovering from a cybersecurity event or incident in accordance with desired recovery time objectives (RTO) and recovery point objectives (RPO).

    (1) Disagree

    (2) Somewhat Disagree

    (3) Somewhat Agree

    (4) Agree

3. The organization maintains a crisis communication plan that manages the organization's reputation after a cybersecurity event or incident occurs.

    (1) Disagree

    (2) Somewhat Disagree

    (3) Somewhat Agree

    (4) Agree

4. **The disaster recovery (DR) and business continuity plan (BCP) is reviewed and updated regularly, at least annually.**
   (1) Disagree
   (2) Somewhat Disagree
   (3) Somewhat Agree
   (4) Agree

RESULTS AND RECOMMENDATIONS

Section 1: Identify Results

SECTION 1: IDENTIFY	SCORE
Question 1	
Question 2	
Question 3	
Question 4	
Question 5	
Question 6	
Question 7	
Question 8	
Total Score	

Section 1: Recommendations

TOTAL SCORE	RECOMMENDATIONS
8-16	The overall ability to identify cybersecurity threats is relatively low. The organization should work to develop a library of information security policies and procedures that will provide the rules and guidance necessary to build an effective cybersecurity program. An inventory of all hardware and software assets should be completed. Once the inventory of assets exists, and there is a clear understanding of scope, a formal risk management process should be implemented so that cybersecurity risks are identified, assigned a risk rating and responded to accordingly. The risk management process will prioritize the implementation of protective controls and defenses based on overall risk appetite. It is important for the organization to clearly understand what regulatory requirements exist regarding cybersecurity so that there is an appreciation for what will need to be accomplished to achieve compliance.

17 - 30	The overall ability to identify cybersecurity threats is inconsistent. The organization may have an incomplete set of information security policies and procedures or, the policies and procedures may not be used properly to govern the cybersecurity program. There may be a partial asset inventory, or an inventory that is not current and needs to be refreshed. A risk management process may exist, but one of several issues may need to be addressed to make the process effective. Potential opportunities to improve the risk management process include: (1) increasing participation amongst data owners and executive stakeholders, (2) increasing the frequency of the risk management exercise, (3) making sure that qualified and credentialed experts perform the risk management exercise, and (4) use the results of the risk management exercise to take actionable steps on improving the overall cybersecurity program. The organization should commit to learning about any and all regulatory requirements pertaining to cybersecurity.
31 - 40	The overall ability to identify cybersecurity threats is very good. The organization has a library of information security policies and procedures that effectively govern the cybersecurity program. There may be an opportunity to review policies and procedures more frequently to ensure they remain current and relevant. The organization maintains a comprehensive inventory of information technology assets. The organization has a formal risk management program and they use the results of this program to prioritize improvements made to the cybersecurity program. The organization has a very good understanding of regulatory requirements regarding cybersecurity.

RESULTS AND RECOMMENDATIONS

Section 2: Protect

SECTION 1: PROTECT	SCORE
Question 1	
Question 2	
Question 3	
Question 4	
Question 5	
Question 6	
Question 7	
Question 8	
Question 9	
Question 10	
Question 11	
Question 12	
Question 13	
Question 14	
Question 15	
Question 16	
Total Score	

Section 2: Recommendations

TOTAL SCORE	RECOMMENDATIONS
16-32	The overall ability of the organization to protect itself against cybersecurity threats and attacks is very low. Many security controls that are required to effectively protect the organization and reduce overall risk are either absent or not configured correctly. The organization should immediately look for opportunities to add security controls or modify existing ones according to the results of the risk management process.
33 - 65	The organization can protect itself against certain types of cybersecurity threats and attacks, but not others. Several types of existing security controls have been implemented effectively, but the overall cybersecurity program could be improved by security controls or modifications to existing security controls according to the results of the risk management process.
65 - 80	The organization is in an excellent position to protect itself from most cybersecurity threats and attacks. Many security controls are implemented and are effective. There is a need to frequently review existing security controls and look for ways to make minor improvements.

RESULTS AND RECOMMENDATIONS

Section 3: Detect

SECTION 1: IDENTIFY	SCORE
Question 1	
Question 2	
Question 3	
Question 4	
Total Score	

Section 3: Detect

TOTAL SCORE	RECOMMENDATIONS
4 -8	The overall ability to detect cybersecurity events and incidents is very low. The organization does not have the capability to know when security controls have been compromised, causing an extreme delay in any detection of an incident and the ability to invoke an incident response plan. The organization should immediately work to understand the normal behaviors of the network and data flow, then work to implement the capability to detect events and incidents.
11 - 17	The organization may be able to detect certain types of cybersecurity security events and incidents, but not all of them. The ability to know when security controls have been compromised is inconsistent and reactive. The organization should immediately work to understand the normal behaviors of the network and data flow, and then work to implement the capability to detect events and incidents.
17 - 20	The organization can effectively detect cybersecurity events and incidents. There may be an opportunity to fine-tune the detection process, procedures and related technologies to reduce the overall number of false positive detections.

RESULTS AND RECOMMENDATIONS

Section 4: Response

SECTION 1: IDENTIFY	SCORE
Question 1	
Question 2	
Question 3	
Question 4	
Question 5	
Question 6	
Total Score	

Section 4: Response

TOTAL SCORE	RECOMMENDATIONS
6 -12	The overall ability to respond to cybersecurity events and incidents is very low. The organization should immediately: (2) develop a formal incident response plan, (3) establish an incident response team and (4) be sure that the organization can effectively mitigate attacks, communicate about incidents properly and effectively preserve forensic evidence.
13 - 25	The organization has some elements of an effective incident response plan in place, but there are opportunities for overall improvement. Employees must understand what their role is in responding to a cybersecurity incident and how to effectively communicate with the organization during a response effort. The organization may also need to improve the overall process used to investigate the cybersecurity event or incident and properly preserve forensic evidence.
25 - 30	The organization can respond effectively to most cybersecurity events and incidents. There may be minor opportunities for improvement to the overall incident response plan, typically in the areas of event or incident investigation and preservation of forensic evidence.

RESULTS AND RECOMMENDATIONS

Section 4: Recover

SECTION 1: IDENTIFY	SCORE
Question 1	
Question 2	
Question 3	
Question 4	
Question 5	
Question 6	
Total Score	

Section 4: Recover

TOTAL SCORE	RECOMMENDATIONS
6 - 12	The overall ability to recover from cybersecurity events and incidents is very low. The organization should immediately develop a formal disaster recovery (DR) and business continuity plan (BCP). The plan should allow for prompt recovery of critical systems and should be reviewed and tested frequently, at least annually.
13 - 25	The organization has some elements of an effective DR / BCP plan, but the plan may not be regularly reviewed and tested – or – the plan may not restore critical assets to an operational state within the desired recovery point objective or recovery time objective.
25 - 30	The organization can effectively recover from most cybersecurity events and incidents. There may be an opportunity to review the DR/BCP plan more frequently and test it for effectiveness, at least annually.

Bonus Material:

Decline of service letter example is to be modified and used at your own risk and discretion.

Date:

Enter client name
and address

RE: Your Company Name, Inc. **Decline of Service**

Enter contact person name

Technology and security needs have evolved over the past few years. Previously, when you had a problem, you called us and we sent someone to resolve the issue. Now more than ever, your business and employees' productivity are linked to your data security and computer network, resulting in effective and efficient business operations. And another thing to consider – the "bad guys" are trying to get into your computer systems. In an effort to provide the best possible protection for our clients, we have proposed our proactive managed services (enter name of product offered), which allows us to monitor and help protect your company's data and computer systems. Even though you subscribe to our Managed BDR (Backup Data Recovery) Service, that is still not enough to protect your company.

Your company has opted to decline our proactive Ultimate Managed Services. Because I feel strongly about our recommendations, and because we are the company you will call if you need help with your data and IT systems, I felt it necessary to put this in writing.

We have designed our proactive Ultimate Managed Services to help prevent and effectively remediate security and network issues. We know the service model you are staying with is inadequate in today's environment, and we can't take the risk of being held liable when we have presented an effective alternative. You acknowledge that you have declined our Ultimate Managed Services and Company Name, Inc. will not be held liable for any damages, technology problems, cyberattacks, lost profits, lost computer usage, interruption of business, or loss of use of client data.

Bonus Material:

Of course, we will be available to support you, should anything go wrong. We will give our best effort to serve you. I do not want there to be any unpleasant surprises or ill will should you have problems related to your computer data and systems.

Best Regards,

Your Name and Title, Account Manager
Your Company Name, Inc.

Client Name,   Authorized Representative

Date

A Final Word…

The reason I published this book was to fortify business owners with the basic knowledge they need to make a great decision when locking down their MSP. I believe we need to better protect ourselves as qualified computer consultants and can contribute to our clients' business success, just as a great marketing consultant, attorney, accountant, or financial advisor can.

The technology industry is ever changing and growing at such a rapid pace that most business owners can't keep up with all of the latest gadgets, alphabet soup acronyms, and choices available to us. Plus, many of the "latest and greatest" technological developments have a shelf life of six months before they become obsolete or completely out-of-date. Sorting through this rapidly moving mess of information to formulate an intelligent plan for growing a business requires a professional, who not only understands technology and how it works, but also understands how people and businesses need to work with technology to make progress.

Unfortunately, the complexity of security technology makes it easy for a business owner to fall victim to self-incompetence.

We've all had those clients who declined to go with our full service, offering only to state later that they pay us to protect them. We have to remind them that the pricing was too high, and they somehow never remember that… When this happens, it creates feelings of mistrust toward all business owners and vendors, which makes it difficult for those of us striving to deliver exceptional value and service to our clients.

Therefore, I encourage you, my fellow MSP, to step up your game, lock down your MSP, take this checklist to market within your own clients, and upsell them on these much-needed services. If you aren't willing to do so, you are doing a disservice to our industry.

I certainly want your feedback on the ideas in this book. If you find missing items on the list, please send me a message so that I may add them to the future updates!

Your contributions, thoughts, and stories will help make it possible. Please write, call or e-mail me with your ideas.

For more resources and more information, please visit:

www.msspplaybook.com

and join us on Facebook via

www.Facebook.com/MSSPPlaybook

for a full list of updated resources and links to ensure that you're finding and making use of the most up-to-date tools and security practices that are available to protect not only your business, but your clients' businesses too.

About the Author

Charles Henson

Charles Henson is a managing partner of Nashville Computer, the premier cybersecurity & IT services firm in Music City. He was featured in Cyber Crime; a documentary made for Amazon Prime. He is an international best-selling author and is often featured in industry publications. He has appeared on the cover of ChannelPro Magazine. An in-demand speaker, he's appeared at business venues around the country, including Chicago, Dallas, New York, Los Angeles, and on many stages in between.

Made in the USA
Columbia, SC
19 July 2020